Red Bananas and Yams

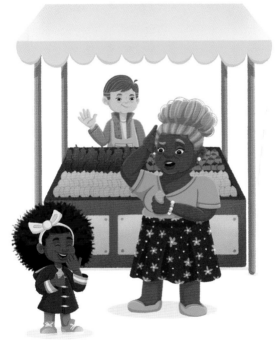

Written by Tony Dallas

Illustrated by Lhaiza Morena

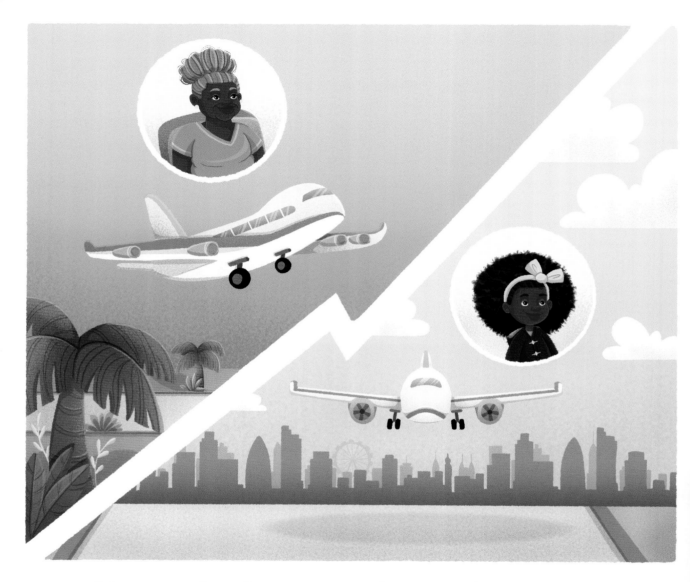

Nana is in Jamaica. She gets
on a jet. Nana will visit me!

We need food. We go to the market.

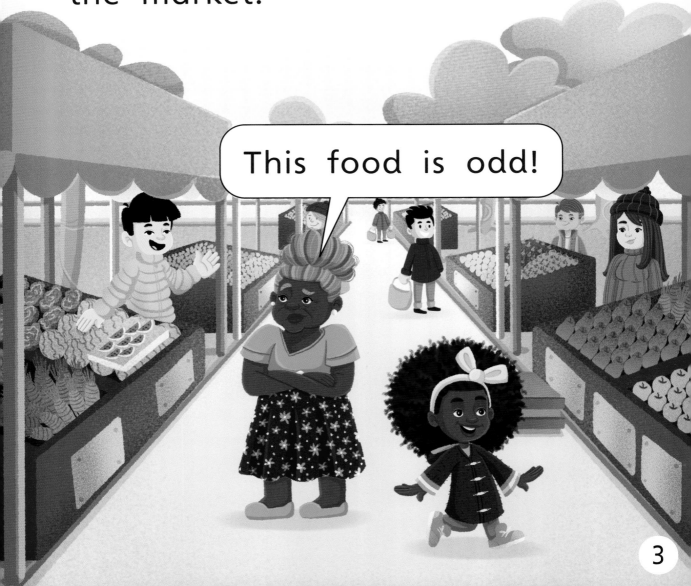

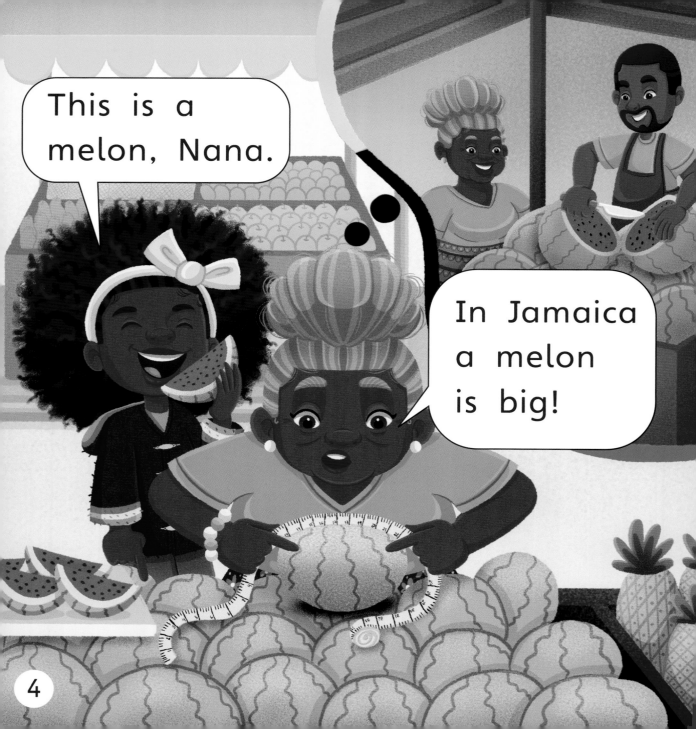

The man turns to look at Nana.

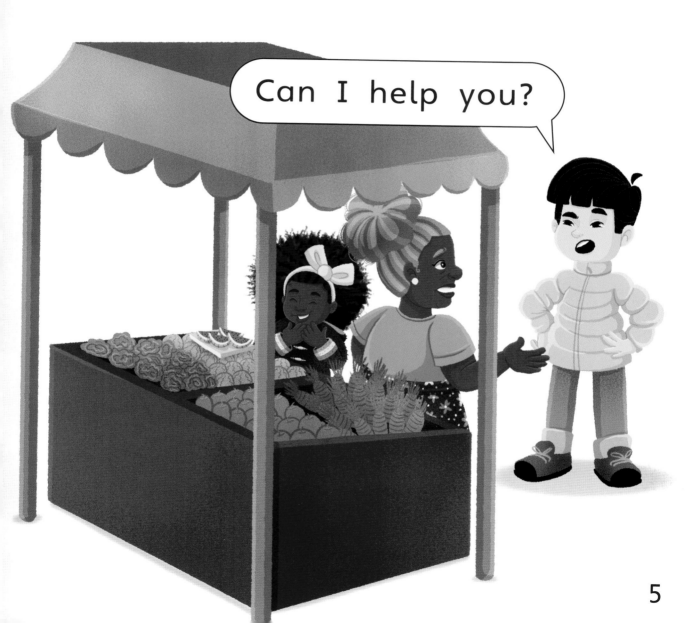

Can I help you?

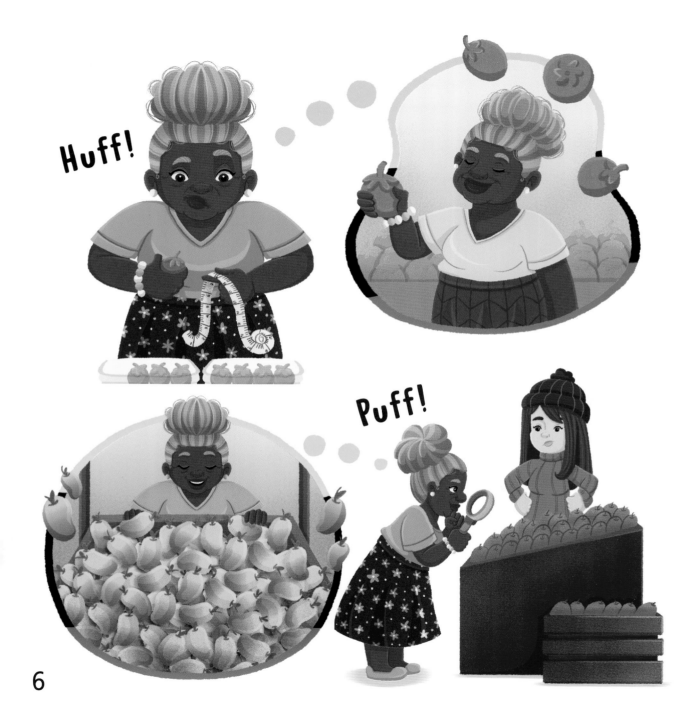

Huff!

Puff!

6

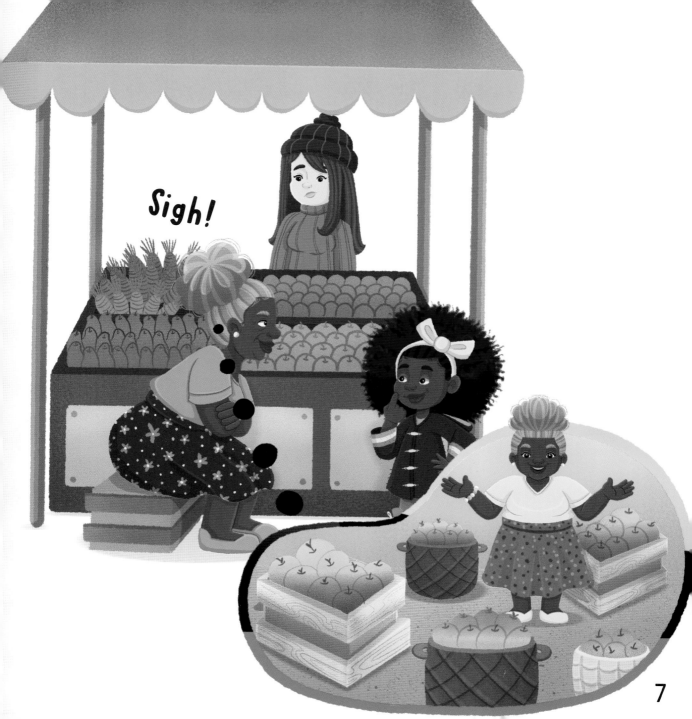

Sigh!

7

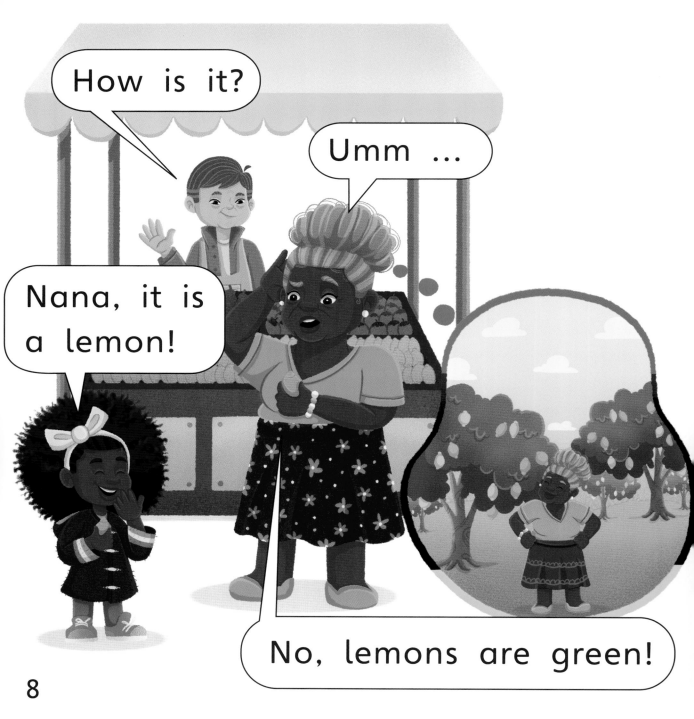

8

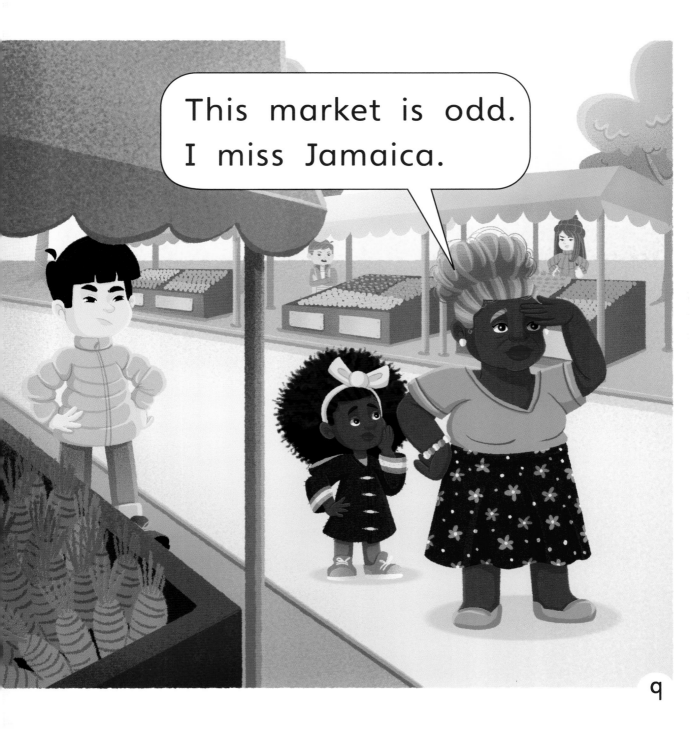

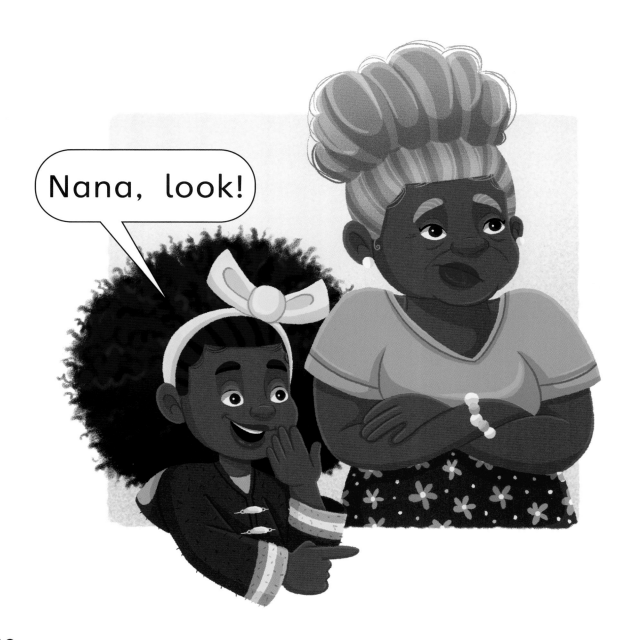

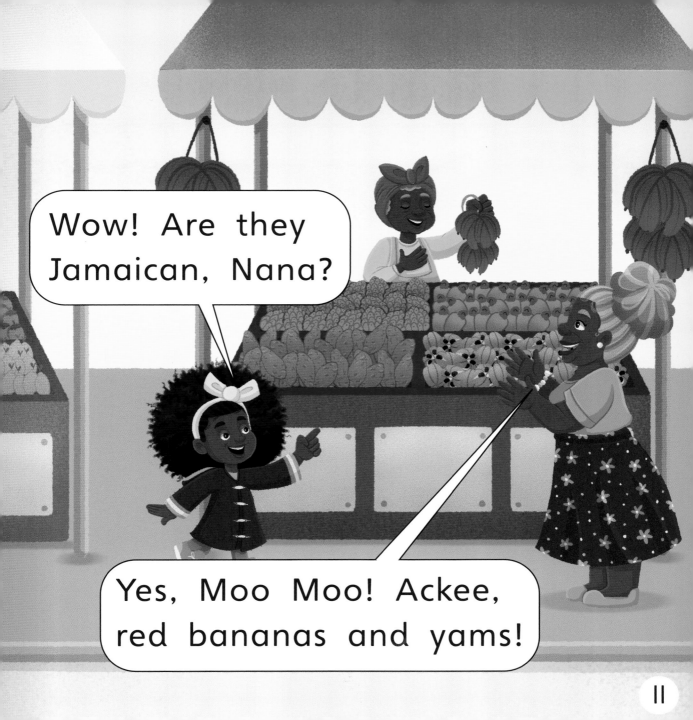

11

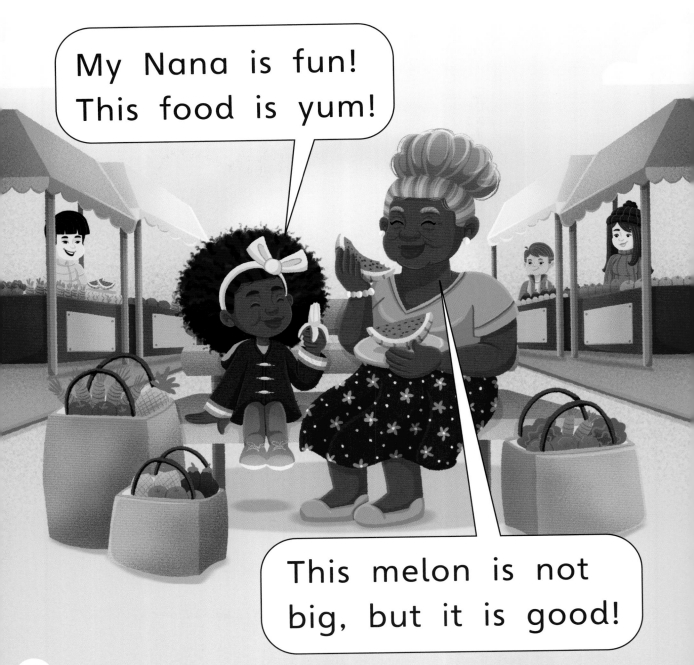